JESUS INVITES ME TO THE FEAST

MY FIRST EUCHARIST JOURNAL

Christine Way Skinner

Liguori

Imprimi Potest:
Harry Grile, CSsR, Provincial
Denver Province, The Redemptorists

Imprimatur: "In accordance with c. 827, permission to publish has been granted on April 14, 2011, by the Most Reverend Robert J. Hermann, Auxiliary Bishop Emeritus, Archdiocese of St. Louis. Permission to publish is an indication that nothing contrary to Church teaching is contained in this work. It does not imply any endorsement of the opinions expressed in the publication; nor is any liability assumed by this permission."

Published by Liguori Publications
Liguori, Missouri 63057

To order, call 800-325-9521
www.liguori.org

Library of Congress Cataloging-in-Publication Data

Skinner, Christine Way.
Jesus invites me to the feast : my first Eucharist journal / Christine Way Skinner.—1st ed.
p. cm.
ISBN 978-0-7648-1998-8
1. First communion—Catholic Church—Juvenile literature. I. Title.
BX2237.S55 2011
264'.0203607—dc22

2011008217

Compliant with *The Roman Missal,* third edition.

Liguori Publications, a nonprofit corporation, is an apostolate of the Redemptorists. To learn more about the Redemptorists, visit Redemptorists.com.

Printed in the United States of America
22 21 20 19 18 / 6 5 4 3 2
First Edition

Cover design: Wendy Barnes
Artwork: Christine Way Skinner, Chris Sharp, and Wendy Barnes

Contents

Acknowledgments

This journal would not have been written were it not for the help and inspiration of many people, including the families of St. John Chrysostom Parish who participated in the first Eucharist preparation in 2005 and 2006, as well as Michael, Alicia, Beth, Oliver, Anna, and Patrick, who all said "I want to draw like you, Mommy" or "That's ugly" at the appropriate moment.

Getting Ready

Jesus has invited you to join him at the feast of the holy Eucharist. For the next few months you will travel an important journey of prayer and learning. At the end, you will be ready to celebrate your first holy Communion and meet Jesus in the sacrament of Eucharist with the rest of your parish family.

As part of your preparation, you will complete this journal at home with your family. When your preparation is complete, not only will you have learned a lot about what this sacrament of Eucharist means, but you will have a wonderful "memory book" to remind you of this special time in your life.

This journey toward your first Eucharist is not a journey you walk by yourself. It is a journey on which you have many, many companions—family, friends, teachers, and members of your parish family. With God as our loving parent, we are all brothers and sisters. We try always to love one another and support one another.

One of the ways we support one another is through prayer. As you prepare for your first Eucharist, here is a prayer you and your family can pray together before your evening meal.

LOVING GOD,
please bless your child

____

[write your name here]

who is preparing for
first holy Communion.
Keep him/her always close to you.
Give him/her the strength and courage
to follow your Son, Jesus.

Throughout the world, children your age are beginning to prepare for their first Eucharist. Use the box below to collect signatures or pictures of other children from your parish who are preparing for this sacrament.

Part One

Our Journey Begins at Baptism

When we first began our journey toward receiving Jesus in the Eucharist, most of us could not even walk. On the first part of our Christian journey, we were carried! Where did that journey begin? At our baptism, that's where.

Let's look back at those first steps you took as a Christian. You and your parents can fill in the following section together.

I came to live on this planet on this day:

From the first day you were born, you were a child of God. But your parents wanted the whole world to know what a special child of God you were, and they also wanted to teach you to be a follower of Jesus. So they brought you to church to become a Christian, a member of the Catholic faith.

The day I was baptized:

The church in which I was baptized:

The priest or deacon who baptized me:

Your parents knew raising a child to be a follower of Jesus would be a big job, so they chose people to help them. The Church calls these people godparents.

My godparents are:

My parents chose them to be my godparents because:

Paste or draw a picture of your baptism on this page.

Place a copy of your baptismal certificate on this page.

The symbols of baptism

The symbols of the sacrament of baptism tell us what the sacrament means.

You have **godparents** because your parents need lots of support and guidance to raise you as a Christian. This is not a job to be done alone!

Draw or paste a picture of your godparents here.

When you were baptized, the presider made the **Sign of the Cross** on your forehead. Your parents and godparents did the same. This reminds us that we are all followers of Jesus.

Then everyone listened to the **Word of God** and offered prayers that we would all be faithful followers of the Gospel.

Draw or paste a picture of someone reading from the holy Bible here.

After listening to God's Word, a **Litany of the Saints** might have been sung to remind us that all the wise and holy people who have gone before us support us in our desire to be Christians.

Next we prayed you would be protected from all evil and harm. The presider anointed you with the **Oil of Catechumens** as a sign of strength. Since oil stains can be permanent, the oil also reminds us of the mark of God's love that stays on our souls forever. God will never abandon us, even if we forget about God.

Ritual Connection

A Litany of the Saints

Leader: Holy Mary, Mother of God,

Response: Pray for us!

Leader: Saint Joseph,

Response: Pray for us!

Leader: All holy men and women,

Response: Pray for us!

The presider then blessed the water that would be poured over your head. He asked if you rejected sin and accepted faith. These are called our **baptismal promises**. If you were baptized as a baby, your parents and godparents answered these questions for you.

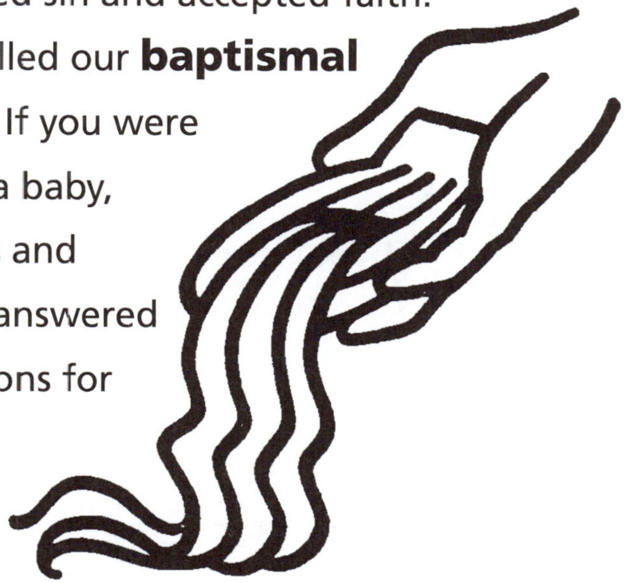

Ritual Connection

Renewing My Baptismal Promises

Leader: Do you say "no" to sin?

Response: I do.

Leader: Do you believe in God the Father, Jesus, his only-begotten Son, the Holy Spirit, and the Church?

Response: I do.

The most important moment of your baptism was when the presider poured **water** over your forehead and baptized you in the name of the Father and of the Son and of the Holy Spirit.

Cut out a picture of water from a magazine and paste it here.

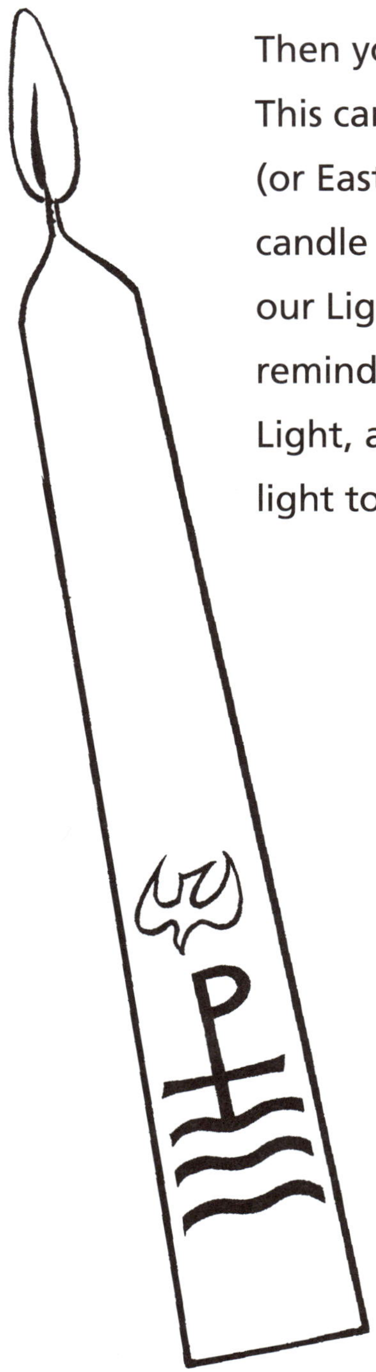

Then you were given a **candle**. This candle is lit from the paschal (or Easter) candle. The paschal candle is the symbol of Jesus our Light. The baptismal candle reminds us that Jesus is our Light, and we should bring his light to the world.

The presider then pointed out the **white garment** you were wearing. This garment reminds us of the new life we all have in Jesus.

With your baptism, you officially became a member of the Church!

God called you by name

Each one of us is unique and special to God. God knows each one of us by our name. God told the prophet Isaiah how very, very precious each one of us is. This is what God said to the people:

> *Do not fear, for I have redeemed you; I have called you by name: you are mine. When you are in danger, I will be with you. I am the Lord, your God. I would trade nations for you. Because you are precious in my eyes and honored, and I love you.*(See Isaiah 43:1–4.)

At your baptism, you were given your name and "officially" called by that name for the first time.

My name is:

____

My name means:

____

____

____

____

Paste a picture or a holy card of your patron saint here.

We Catholics have a tradition of naming our children after people we look up to because they have been faithful followers of Jesus. These people are called *saints*. Do you share the name of a saint? If you have a picture or a holy card with your patron saint on it, paste it in the box. If you do not share the name of a saint, look for a saint who shares your birthday.

My patron saint is:

____

Write something about your patron saint here:

____

____

____

Use this page to paste in more pictures of your patron saint or other holy people who are good examples to you of people who have followed Jesus faithfully.

God called people in the Bible

When God called you to be a member of the Church, you joined a long line of people God has chosen and called. You can find the stories of some of these people in the Bible. It may surprise you to learn that some of them are children your age.

Ask your parents to help you look up some of these stories in the Bible. Some of the stories might be easier to understand if you read them from a children's version of the Bible.

God calls Abraham and Sarah
Genesis 12:1–6

God calls Moses
Exodus 3:2–14

God calls the boy Samuel
1 Samuel 3:1–11

God calls the boy David to be king
1 Samuel 16:1–23

God calls the boy Jeremiah
Jeremiah 1:4–10

Jesus calls the first apostles
Matthew 4:18–23

Jesus calls Saint Paul
Acts 9:1–22

We are members of Christ's body

Saint Paul tells us in his letter to the people of Rome:

> ***We, though many,***
> ***are one body in Christ.***
> **Romans 12:5**

When we were baptized, we became members of the Church, which is Christ's body on earth.

Some artists have tried to show this by drawing Jesus' body made up of many people.

Color the picture on this page. Choose one of the bodies to represent you, and color that one in your favorite color.

Jesus Invites You to the Banquet Table

When you were baptized, you became a member of Christ's body—the Church. Now that you are older, Jesus invites you to join him at the banquet table. At the table of the Lord, you and all the other members of Jesus' Church will be fed with the Body and Blood of Christ. This is called **Eucharist,** or **holy Communion**.

We celebrate Eucharist together every **Sunday**. We call Sunday **The Lord's Day**. Christians everywhere keep that day holy because it is the day Jesus rose from the dead. We gather each week to remember what he did for us and to meet him again in the celebration of the Eucharist, or the **Mass.**

Ritual Connection

The Church celebrates the Eucharist every day of the week even though most people only attend on Sundays. During this special year while you are preparing for your first Eucharist, ask your parents to take you to a weekday Mass. What differences do you see between the weekday celebrations and the celebrations on Sunday?

Families celebrate the holiness of Sunday in many ways. Some people have special meals after Mass. Some families take walks together or visit with family.

Circle some of the ways in which your family celebrates Sunday. Write in your own activities if they are not listed.

- Going to Mass
- Visiting with family
- Eating a special meal
- Resting
- Taking a walk
- Having a special treat
- Staying home from work
- Reading a story about a saint
- Reading a Bible story

____

____

____

____

We love to celebrate!

All over the world, people gather to celebrate birthdays, holidays, and anniversaries. People gather to celebrate holy days and the changing of seasons. Sometimes people celebrate just because they feel like celebrating.

Draw or paste a picture of one of your family celebrations here.

Almost every celebration has four parts:

Gathering Together

Sharing Stories

Sharing Food and Gifts

Saying Goodbye

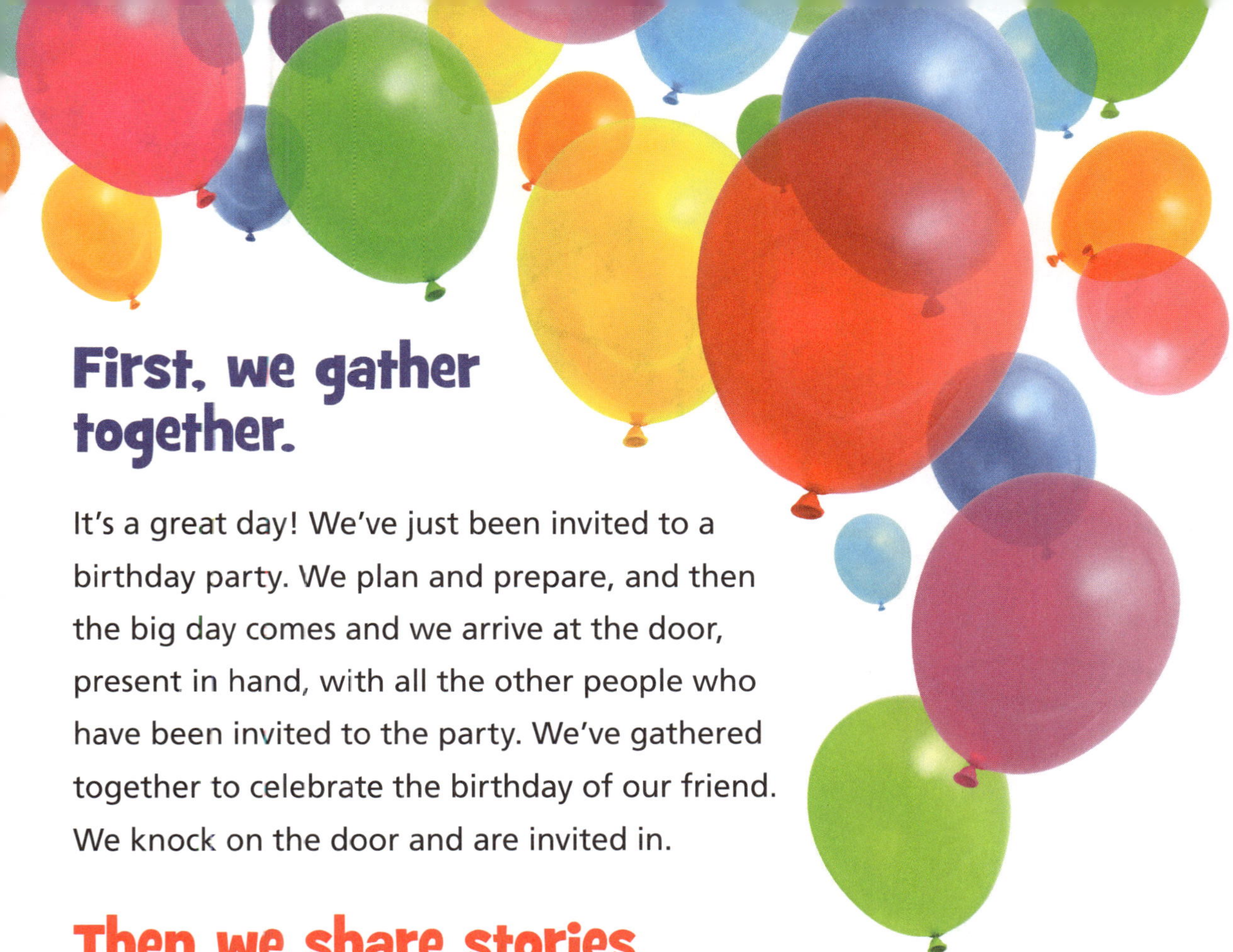

First, we gather together.

It's a great day! We've just been invited to a birthday party. We plan and prepare, and then the big day comes and we arrive at the door, present in hand, with all the other people who have been invited to the party. We've gathered together to celebrate the birthday of our friend. We knock on the door and are invited in.

Then we share stories.

Once we are in the door, our host or hostess tells us what to do: "You may put your coat here. The gifts go here." After we are settled, we are introduced to the people we don't know and learn a little bit about one another. We ask our friends what they have been doing since the last time we saw them, and we tell them what we have been doing. Finally, the host or hostess tells us what is going to happen at the party, what the rules of the games are, and when we are going to open gifts and eat food. We must listen while all these things happen or we will not know what to do and when to do it.

We celebrate by sharing food and gifts.

Two things we can count on at a birthday party are gifts and food. A birthday party without these two things wouldn't feel much like a birthday party. We have come to celebrate our friend's birthday, and so we sing to her or him and give gifts to show that we care for our friend. Then we all share a meal together.

We say goodbye.

Finally, it is time to wrap up our celebration and return home to our ordinary lives.

Color the picture.

When we leave, our hearts are happier, our friendships are deeper, and our tummies are fuller than when we arrived.

Jesus also invites us to a *celebration*

This celebration is called Eucharist. Let's look at what we do at our celebration of the Eucharist.

First, we *gather together.*

It's **Sunday**—a great day! We're invited to a celebration of the resurrection of Jesus Christ. The invitation comes from God. We have come to celebrate the rising of our friend Jesus from the dead. We don't need to knock when we come to this place because we all come as sisters and brothers. The church is our home.

As we enter the church, we bless ourselves with holy water. This reminds us that we became part of this family at our baptism. Every time we gather together in his name, Jesus becomes present among us.

Once we've gathered, we sit down to *share the story of God's love.*

The **ministers of the Word** and the **priest** proclaim the Word of God to us. The readings are taken from our book of sacred **Scriptures** called the Bible. These are put into a special book, called a ***Lectionary,*** for us to use at Mass.

We listen to God's Word so that we know how much God loves us and how to live as followers of God's Son, Jesus.

The main event at our celebration of the Eucharist is *sharing a sacred meal.*

Just like at a birthday party, we **offer gifts and share food**. The gifts we bring are simple bread and wine. We offer them to God and give them to the priest to bless. Unlike at any other kind of party, however, our gifts are returned to us! They are not the same though—they have been changed. They are returned to us as the Body and Blood of Jesus. This becomes our spiritual meal.

Finally, it is time to say goodbye and return home.

We go in peace to love and serve the Lord. When we leave, our hearts are happier, our friendships are deeper, and our spirits are fed by the sacred food of the Eucharist. We call all of this action **liturgy**. The word *liturgy* means "the work of the people." Let's look more closely at what we do in our Sunday work.

Jesus is here! Christ is in our midst!

The Church teaches that when we gather together for Mass, Christ is truly present among us in four important ways. In the boxes below, draw a picture of the places where we meet Jesus in our celebration.

Christ is present in the Word

The Word became flesh and made his dwelling among us. JOHN 1:14

Christ is present in the priest

You are a priest forever according to the order of Melchizedek. HEBREWS 7:17

Christ is present in the sacrament

This is my body, which will be given for you. LUKE 22:19

Christ is present in the people

Where two or three are gathered together in my name, there am I. MATTHEW 18:20

We Gather Together

As Catholics, we believe that when we gather together with others, Jesus becomes really and truly present in our gathering. He told us, “Where two or three are gathered…there am I” (Matthew 18:20). This is why the Church spends a lot of time at the beginning of each eucharistic celebration helping to unite all the people who have come to Mass to give thanks and praise to God.

The People of God gather together during the **Introductory Rites**. These prayers and actions help us recognize that we are all one people. Here are the parts of the Introductory Rites:

Opening Hymn

We sing a gathering song.

Our many different voices are joined as one in song.

Entrance Procession

As the procession moves up through the people we are drawn together, and our eyes all meet in one place.

Sign of the Cross

We all make the Sign of the Cross together. Our unity is in Jesus.

Greeting

The presider greets us, "The Lord be with you."

We respond as one people, "And with your spirit!"

Penitential Act

We say we are sorry for our sins.

"Lord, have mercy; Christ, have mercy."

Opening Prayer

The presider begins with the words, "Let us pray..."

We sing a gathering song—our voices are one

At this celebration of Eucharist, we also sing. The songs we sing are songs of joy and praise to God. When we all sing together, we can hear and feel that we are one body.

Write the name of some of your favorite "church" songs here.

Ritual Connection

Try singing a song together for your family prayer. You could do this for your morning or evening prayer. Grace before meals is also a good time to use sung prayer.

Gathered together under the cross of Jesus

Then the ministers who will be leading our liturgy process in. All of our eyes meet in one place. What leads our procession? It is the cross of Jesus.

Then all together we make the Sign of the Cross. When we make this sign, we say to the world and to one another that we are gathering as one family with God as our father, Jesus as our brother, and the Holy Spirit who sanctifies us.

Decorate the border of the Sign of the Cross prayer to show it is a very special sign of who we are as followers of Jesus. You might want to use crosses in your design.

The Sign of the Cross

In the name
of the Father,
and of the Son,
and of the
Holy Spirit.

We are a broken body

When we gather together under the cross, we remember that Jesus died because of people's sins. Jesus wants us to live like he did. He wants us to take care of one another and love one another. This is not always easy to do. Most of us would rather keep what is ours instead of sharing it with others. We would rather do what we want to do instead of what our parents or teachers want us to do. It is easier for us to say the mean things we think when we are angry instead of being quiet or even saying something kind. When we do the right thing even when it is difficult, we are being like Jesus. We are "taking up our cross and following him."

Sometimes it is not easy to live as Jesus wants us to live. We are selfish, mean, or unloving. When we are not as loving as we should be, the body of Christ is broken. This is why at the beginning of Mass we ask for God's mercy. We think of the ways in which we have not been loving. This is called the **Penitential Act**. We say, "Lord, have mercy. Christ, have mercy. Lord, have mercy." Sometimes we say a prayer called the *Confiteor.* In this prayer we say we are sorry for all the things we have done or not done that hurt the body of Christ.

The good news is that Jesus always forgives us. God is merciful!

Ritual Connection

Pray this prayer at bedtime

For the times I have been selfish,
Lord, have mercy.
For the times I have been dishonest,
Christ, have mercy.
For the times I have been unloving,
Lord, have mercy.

Try to think of something you find difficult to do. Write it on the lines of the prayer below. You can say this prayer every time you need God's help to do the right thing.

Dear Jesus,

Sometimes it is hard for me to be loving.

It is especially hard for me to:

____

____

____

Please help me.

Your friend,

The cross

When you are having a hard time "taking up your cross," this story may help remind you that God will never ask us to do more than we are able to do.

A young girl was feeling tired and sad. She fell to her knees in prayer. "O Lord, I can't go on," she said. "My cross is too heavy to bear." The Lord looked at her and replied, "My child, if it is too heavy, pass it to me." Then the Lord showed the girl a door, "Open that door and enter the room. Inside, you will find many different crosses. Pick any cross you wish. Do not choose any cross that is too difficult, but do not choose a cross that is too easy, either." The girl was very relieved and said, "Thank you, Lord" and put down her cross. She entered the door and saw many crosses. Some were so large the tops were not visible. Some were as small as toothpicks. Then she spotted a small cross leaning against a far wall. "I'd like to have that one," she whispered to the Lord. The Lord smiled at the girl and said, "My child, you have chosen the perfect cross. That is the cross you brought here today."

We have one another

When Jesus was carrying his cross to Calvary, he needed help. The soldiers chose a man from the crowd whose name was Simon. A stranger helped lighten Jesus' heavy load.

When we gather together on Sunday for Eucharist, we admit that if Jesus could not carry his cross alone, then neither can we. We cannot celebrate alone. We cannot be kind and loving alone. We cannot bear our burdens alone. We cannot do the hard work of being faithful followers of Jesus alone. We need one another.

Draw or paste a picture of yourself sitting in the church pews with some of the people who help you be a faithful follower of Jesus. These may be members of your family, friends, or even complete strangers like Simon.

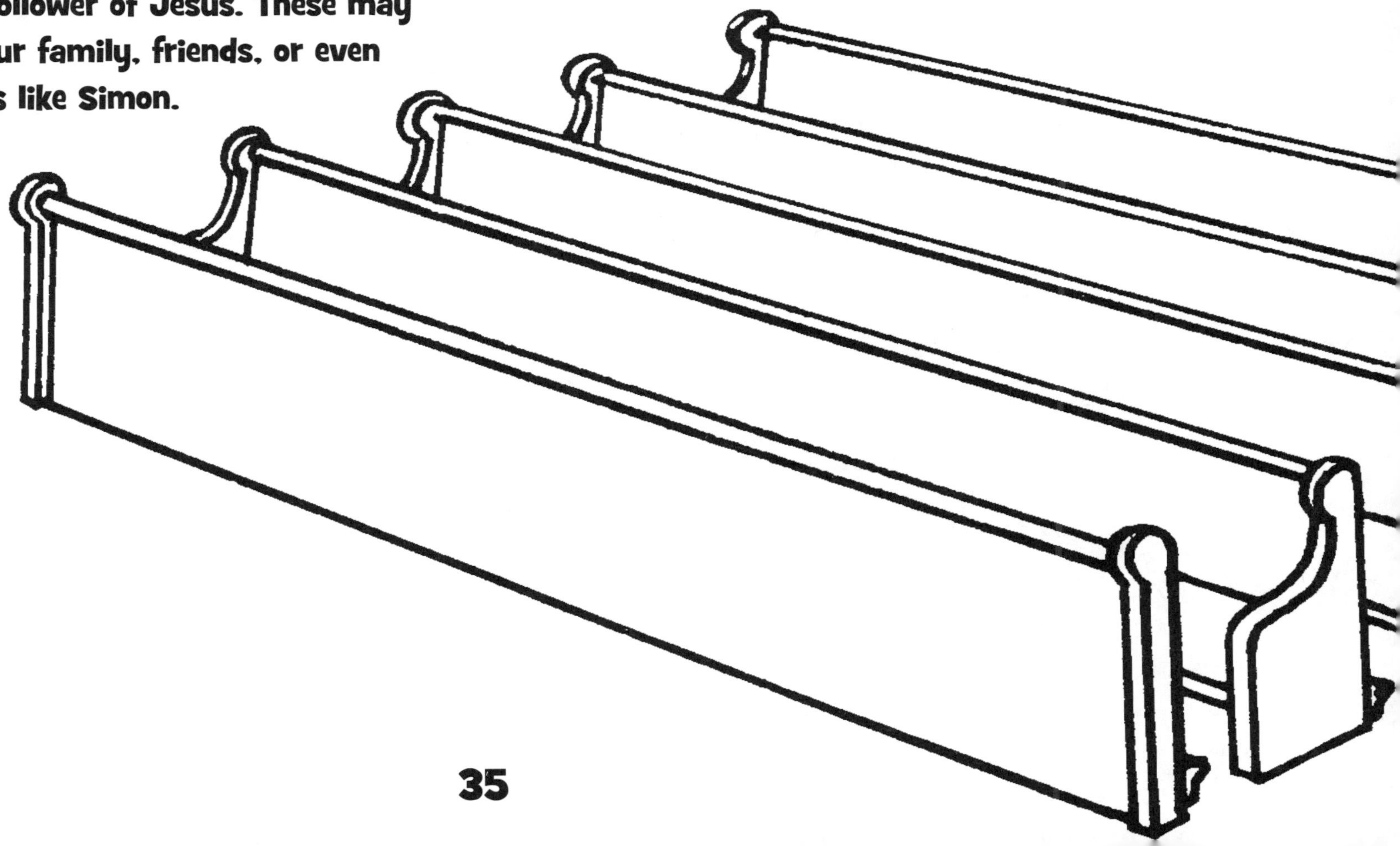

Learn to know and follow Christ

When older children and adults are preparing for baptism, they are blessed using a special ritual. The Sign of the Cross is made over their whole body, and the Church asks Jesus to give them strength.

Ritual Connection

You can use this prayer yourself. Have your parents make the Sign of the Cross over you and say these prayers. To make the prayer even more personal, take photos of your ears, eyes, lips, and feet, and paste them in the circles. You can also draw your body parts in the circles.

Receive the cross on your forehead. It is Christ who now strengthens you with this sign of his love.

What can you do to keep Jesus in your thoughts?

Receive the sign of the cross on your ears, that you may hear the voice of the Lord.

What can you do to listen better to God?

Receive the sign of the cross on your eyes, that you may see the glory of God.

How can your eyes help you know Jesus better?

Receive the sign of the cross on your lips, that you may always speak words of kindness and peace.

How can you show God's love with your speech?

Receive the sign of the cross over your heart, that you may love as Jesus loved.

How can you be more loving?

Receive the sign of the cross on your hands, that Christ may be known in the work you do.

What can you do with your hands to serve God and others?

Receive the sign of the cross over your shoulders, that you may have the strength to carry the crosses of life.

When do you need God to give you strength?

Receive the sign of the cross on your feet, that you may walk in the paths of the Lord.

How can you walk in God's pathways?

My dear children, as we traced the sign of the cross on your forehead, God signed you in your hearts. All through your life, the cross will remind you of God's great love for you.

The cross is a sign of hope

When we look at the cross as Christians, we are not sad. We know that even though Jesus died on the cross, he rose again and lives with God forever. We also know that he did this so that we also may live forever. In the village of La Palma, El Salvador, the people live in great poverty. Still, they have a joyful, hopeful faith. One way they express their faith is to make beautiful artwork. The cross on this page is made in the style of the people of the village of La Palma. Color it in bright, joyful colors.

We Share Sacred Stories

Once all the people have gathered together, it is time for us to sit down and listen to what God has to say to us. This time is called the **Liturgy of the Word**. We believe we really and truly meet Jesus in the holy Scriptures. In the Gospel of John, Jesus is called the "Word [who] became flesh."

Draw or paste a beautiful copy of a Bible here.

These are the parts of the Liturgy of the Word:

First Reading

We hear the stories and wisdom of our great- great- great- great-grandparents in faith.

Psalm

We sing a prayer to God.

Second Reading

The first Christians tell us about God's love.

Gospel Acclamation

We proclaim "Alleluia," which comes from the Hebrew word that means "Praise the Lord."

Gospel

We hear the Good News about Jesus from one of the four Evangelists: Matthew, Mark, Luke, or John.

Homily

The priest helps us understand the meaning of God's Word for our lives today.

Creed

We state the truths of our Catholic faith to which we willingly adhere.

Prayer of the Faithful

We offer the prayers of our community to God. We always pray for ourselves, for the Church, for the needs of the world, and for those people who are sick and those who have died.

The Sower   Luke 8:5-15

Jesus often told parables to teach people about their faith. A parable is a kind of story that teaches a lesson. Here is a parable Jesus told about listening to God's Word.

> *"A sower went out to sow his seed. And as he sowed, some seed fell on the path and was trampled, and the birds of the sky ate it up. Some seed fell on rocky ground, and when it grew, it withered for lack of moisture. Some seed fell among thorns, and the thorns grew with it and choked it. And some seed fell on good soil, and when it grew, it produced fruit a hundredfold."*
>
> *After saying this, he called out, "Whoever has ears to hear ought to hear."*

Not everyone understood what Jesus was talking about. The disciples asked him what the story meant, so he explained the parable to them.

"The seed is the word of God." He said that some people hear God's Word and believe it, but it is taken away from them before it can take root in their hearts.

Other people hear God's Word, but they give up trying to live it as soon as it becomes difficult.

Others care so much about unimportant things that they forget about God's Word. The things that don't matter are like weeds that choke out the things that really do matter in our lives.

Thankfully, the "seed" of God's Word also falls on good soil. When we take good care of our faith in God, our hearts are like the good soil. God's Word grows and spreads and changes the hearts of everyone it touches. Prayer and loving actions are like water to the seeds of God's Word in us. They keep it strong and healthy. We need to take care of our faith in God's Word to help it live strongly within us.

What loving actions can you do to help the plants grow? Write them above the sprouting seeds.

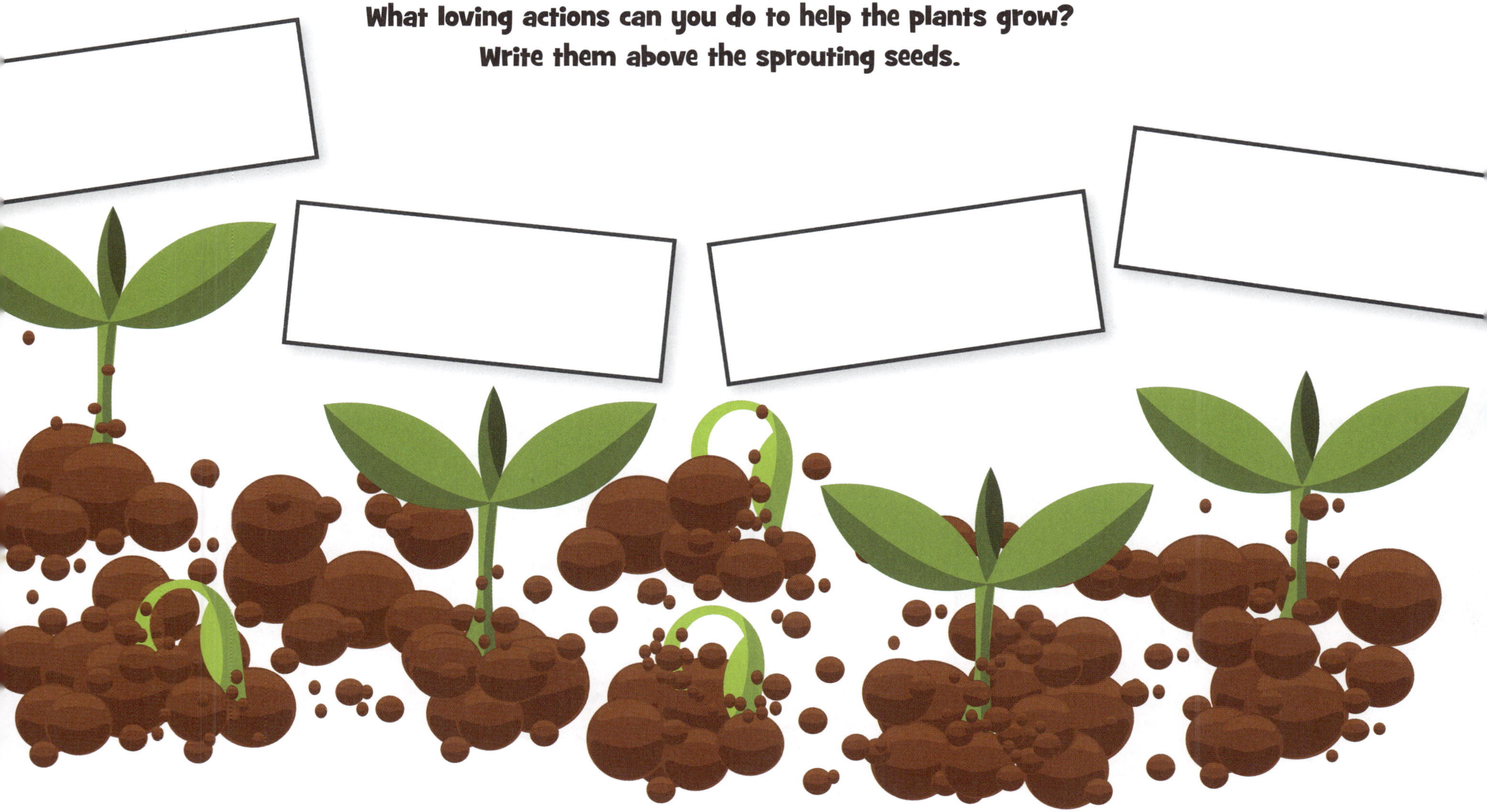

One of the most important things we need to do to hear God's Word is to have some quiet time to listen to God. The words *listen* and *silent* contain exactly the same letters. Perhaps this is not a coincidence. As you color in the letters, think about how we cannot listen if we are never silent.

LISTEN

SILENT

One-minute meditations

The best way to be sure to hear God's Word is to make time every day for prayer. One way to do that is the "one-minute meditation."

Each evening before you go to bed, close your eyes and listen for God's voice. At times, God's voice can be very hard to hear. We have to listen with our hearts and not our ears. God can speak to us through prayer or through the people around us. Acts of kindness and simple prayers are some of the ways in which we hear God's voice.

Practice listening to God for one whole week. Use the chart on page 46 to record some of God's messages to you. Begin your prayer by saying, "Open my heart to hear your Word."

One-minute meditations

On **Sunday**, I listened for God's voice and heard:	
On **Monday**, I listened for God's voice and heard:	
On **Tuesday**, I listened for God's voice and heard:	
On **Wednesday**, I listened for God's voice and heard:	
On **Thursday**, I listened for God's voice and heard:	
On **Friday**, I listened for God's voice and heard:	
On **Saturday**, I listened for God's voice and heard:	

The Bible: God's Word

The **Bible** is the book of God's Word. The Bible is made up of many different writings. In fact, the word *Bible* comes from a word that means "books." The books of the Bible were written in many different ways and at different times. Some of the books are songs, prayers, or poetry. Some are stories. Many books in the Bible tell us about the history of our fathers and mothers in faith.

When we read the Bible in church, we use a ***Lectionary***. The *Lectionary* tells us which Scripture readings we should read each Sunday.

The people who proclaim God's Word to us at Mass are called **ministers of the Word,** or **lectors**. They are called to share God's Word with the people.

The first reading usually comes from the **Old Testament**. Then we sing a **psalm,** which is a sung prayer from the Bible. The person who leads the psalm is called a **cantor.** The second reading is from the **New Testament,** which are stories of the early Christians or letters from the first leaders of the Church to the people.

We save our most important reading—the **Gospel**—for last. We read the stories of Jesus from the four Gospels written by **Matthew**, **Mark**, **Luke**, and **John**. This reading is so important that we sing an **acclamation** before we listen to it.

After we hear all the readings, the **priest** gives a **homily.** The homily helps us understand the meaning of the day's **Scripture**.

After the homily, we say the **Creed** together, and then offer our **prayers of petition,** asking God for the things we need.

Here is a picture for you to color of a minister of the Word proclaiming God's Word to the people at Mass.

Bible Word Search

ACCLAMATION
BIBLE
CANTOR
CREED
FIRST READING
GOD'S WORD
GOSPEL
HOMILY
JOHN
LECTIONARY
LECTOR
LUKE
MARK
MATTHEW
NEW TESTAMENT
OLD TESTAMENT
PETITIONS
PRIEST
PSALM
SCRIPTURE
SECOND READING

Y	Y	E	G	A	E	W	P	U	C	H	E	C	D	L
L	T	Y	T	N	C	R	G	S	N	O	B	A	R	E
I	C	S	N	U	I	C	U	O	A	Y	S	N	O	C
M	R	N	E	Q	C	D	L	T	S	L	D	T	W	T
O	E	H	M	I	D	K	A	A	P	P	M	O	S	I
H	E	O	A	K	R	A	M	E	M	I	E	R	D	O
T	D	J	T	L	U	P	C	A	R	A	R	L	O	N
D	N	T	S	B	I	B	L	E	V	T	T	C	G	A
L	L	L	E	R	O	T	C	E	L	N	S	I	S	R
N	E	W	T	E	S	T	A	M	E	N	T	R	O	Y
G	N	I	D	A	E	R	D	N	O	C	E	S	I	N
E	O	Z	L	S	N	O	I	T	I	T	E	P	S	F
P	K	X	O	N	S	Z	M	A	T	T	H	E	W	T
Z	L	U	K	E	F	P	X	W	S	M	X	R	U	X

Many people have favorite stories or quotations from the Bible. Do you have a favorite story or quotation? If so, draw or copy it in the box to the right. If not, ask your mom or dad if they have a favorite one they could suggest to you.

My favorite Bible story

Finding your way in the Bible

The Bible is divided into small parts so that we can find what we are looking for. First, it is divided into different **books**. Then each book is divided into **chapters**. Finally, each chapter is divided into **verses**.

Book	Chapter	Verse
Genesis	1:	30

The references in this puzzle refer to the colors mentioned in the *New Revised Standard Version (NRSV)* of the Bible.

Look up the Bible verse below to find out which color to use in each section. You will probably need your parents' help.

1. Exodus 28:31
2. Genesis 25:25
3. Judges 5:10
4. Leviticus 13:32
5. Proverbs 16:31
6. Exodus 30:4
7. Song of Solomon 2:1
8. 1 Kings 14:23
9. Matthew 16:2
10. Luke 16:19
11. Revelation 1:13
12. Lamentations 4:5
13. Numbers 33:10
14. Exodus 39:31
15. Genesis 1:30
16. Ecclesiastes 9:8
17. Leviticus 13:30

We Share a Sacred Meal

We have gathered the people of God together. We have listened to God's Word. Now we are ready for the most important part of our celebration. This is called the **Liturgy of the Eucharist**. It is the heart of what we do on Sunday. At this time we give thanks and praise for all God has done for us. We offer all that we have and all that we are to Jesus, and we remember Jesus' Last Supper with his friends.

These are the parts of the Liturgy of the Eucharist.

Preparation of the Gifts

We offer gifts of bread and wine and ourselves to God. The priest or deacon prepares the altar.

Prayer Over the Gifts

On behalf of the community, the priest asks God to make our gifts holy.

Eucharistic Prayer

We offer a great prayer of praise and thanksgiving to God. We tell the story of Jesus' last meal with his friends. We proclaim what we believe.

The Lord's Prayer

We pray the prayer Jesus taught.

Sign of Peace

We offer one another a sign of peace.

Breaking of the Bread

We sing the Lamb of God as the bread is broken to be shared.

Communion

We eat and drink the Body and Blood of Christ. We sing and pray.

The gift of Jesus

Whenever someone gives us a gift, they give us a part of themselves. Every time we look at that gift, we remember the person who gave it to us. In a way, they become present to us again.

What is the most special gift you've ever received?

____

Who gave it to you?

____

Draw or paste a picture of this special gift in the box.

When Jesus was about to die, he wanted to give his disciples a very special gift to remember him by. He gave them the gift at his last meal with them. The gift was not a thing; it was Jesus Christ himself. It was the Eucharist. Jesus gave this gift to all his disciples—from the ones who were present at the meal to us today.

Every time we celebrate the Eucharist, Jesus becomes present to us Body and Blood, Soul and Divinity, in the form of bread and wine. Every time we receive the Body and Blood of Christ at Mass, Jesus gives us the gift of himself again.

What an amazing gift!

Draw a picture of Jesus sharing himself in the form of bread and wine with his disciples.

The story of the Last Supper

During the Eucharistic Prayer, we tell the story of the Last Supper, where Jesus gave this great gift to his friends:

The night before Jesus died, he celebrated a meal with his friends. While they were eating, he took a loaf of bread, blessed it, and shared it with them, saying, "Take and eat, for this is my Body."

Then he took a cup. He gave thanks to God and shared it with them. Everyone drank from it. Jesus said to them, "Take and drink, for this is my Blood."

He said, "Do this in memory of me."

Here is a picture of the Last Supper for you to color.

After supper, Jesus talked to his friends for a long time. He told them how much he loved them and how much God loved them too.

Then Jesus did something astonishing: he washed their feet! He told his disciples if they wanted to be his followers, they would have to serve one another the same way he had served them.

He said to them, "Love one another as I have loved you."

If we want to be true followers of Jesus, we, too, must love as Jesus loved. We must serve one another. This means that sometimes

- when it is not our turn to pick up the toys, we can do it anyway just to be kind.
- when someone in our family is sick, we can bring them apple juice or a warm blanket.
- when we are finished doing our schoolwork, we can help a friend who is having trouble with his or hers.

As followers of Jesus, we can serve one another in many different ways. Think of a few ways in which you can serve the people around you, and write them in the space provided. Then don't forget to do them!

I can serve my family by: ______________________

____

I can serve my friends by: ______________________

____

I can serve my world by: ______________________

____

The first Christians remember Jesus

After Jesus died and rose to new life, his friends remembered what he had done at the Last Supper. They remembered how he had taken bread and the cup and gave thanks. They remembered how he'd broken the bread, poured the wine, and gave it to them. They remembered how he'd washed their feet.

His friends also remembered Jesus' words, **"Do this in memory of me."** And so they came together in their homes. They took bread and wine. They gave thanks, broke the bread, poured the wine, and shared it. When they did this, they knew Jesus was with them.

We remember Jesus

Like the very first Christians, we remember Jesus' words, "Do this in memory of me." Every time we eat and drink the Body and Blood of Christ at Mass, we do it in memory of Jesus. Now, more than two thousand years after Jesus' birth, he is still present to us when we celebrate Eucharist.

Color the border around these special words.

Bread baking

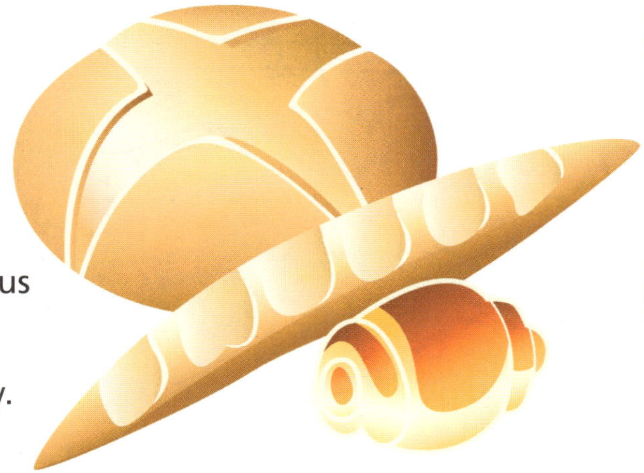

In the time of Jesus (and in many places today) people baked their own bread. Jesus may have even helped his own mother knead the bread when he was a small boy. Is someone in your family a good cook? Ask them to help you make some homemade bread, and share it with your family.

Here is a recipe you can use if you do not have a family favorite:

Ingredients:

2-1/4 cups of milk
2 packages of yeast
1/2 cup warm water
2 tablespoons shortening
1 tablespoon salt
2-3/4 cups white flour
1/3 cup honey
2-3/4 cups whole wheat flour

Directions:

- Dissolve the yeast in the warm water.
- Scald the milk and let it cool.
- Mix the milk with the other ingredients.
- Knead the dough.
- Let it rise in a warm place until double its size.
- Shape the bread into loaves.
- Let it rise again.
- Bake at 400° for 20 minutes.

Here are some questions to talk about while you wait for your bread to rise and bake.

Why do you think Jesus chose bread as a sign to remember him by?

Yeast is the ingredient that makes the bread rise. Saint Paul tells us that Christians are supposed to be like yeast in the world. What do you think he meant?

Jesus said, "I am the Bread of Life." What do you think he meant?

Eucharist: Giving thanks and praise

The word *Eucharist* comes from a Greek word that means "to give thanks." When we celebrate Mass, we are thanking God for everything God has ever given us. The gifts of bread and wine that we bring to the altar remind us of all these gifts. The greatest of these gifts is Jesus. God gives us wheat. We take that wheat and our imagination and creativity and make bread. **THANK YOU, GOD!** We offer that bread to God when we present the gifts at Mass.

The priest says, "Blessed are you, Lord God of all creation, for through your goodness we have received the bread we offer you: fruit of the earth and work of human hands, it will become for us the bread of life." God takes the bread and gives it back to us as the Body of Jesus. **WE GIVE THANKS AND PRAISE TO GOD!**

God gives us grapes. We take those grapes and our imagination and creativity and make wine. **THANK YOU, GOD!** We offer that wine to God when we present the gifts at Mass. The priest says, "Blessed are you, Lord God of all creation, for through your goodness we have received the wine we offer you: fruit of the vine and work of human hands, it will become our spiritual drink." God takes the wine and gives it back to us as the Blood of Jesus. **WE GIVE THANKS AND PRAISE TO GOD!**

It is not only at Mass that we should give thanks and praise to God. We must say "thanks" every day. Here is a Prayer of Thanksgiving you can say to tell God that you are grateful for all God has done for you. You can color in the border with pictures of things for which you are thankful.

A Thanksgiving Prayer

Loving God, we praise and thank you for all the wonderful things you have given us. We thank you for the earth that gives us wheat and grapes and all kinds of food for our bodies. We thank you for the human hands that make the wheat into bread, the grapes into wine, and the good things of the earth into things we can use. We thank you for the gift of your Spirit, who gathers us together as your family to share your love.

We pray the prayer Jesus taught

Just before we receive Communion, we pray together the prayer Jesus taught. Every Christian should know this prayer by heart. If you do not know it, this is a good time to memorize it.

Color the border around the prayer that Jesus taught us.

Our Father, who art in heaven,
hallowed be thy name;
thy kingdom come,
thy will be done
on earth as it is in heaven.
Give us this day
our daily bread,
and forgive us our trespasses
as we forgive those
who trespass against us;
and lead us not into temptation,
but deliver us from evil. Amen.

Loaves and Fishes

At Communion, our spirits are fed with the Bread of Life. Jesus not only cared about people's spirits, he was also concerned about people whose bodies were hungry. The Gospels are filled with stories about the hungry being fed. Here is one of those stories:

A very large crowd had followed Jesus to the Sea of Galilee. They had seen some of the amazing things he had been doing and wanted to learn more about him.

Ritual Connection

Catholics are obliged to fast for an hour before receiving holy Communion. We do this so that the hunger we feel in our bodies will remind us that our spirit hungers also. It is easier to remember to feed our bodies than our spirits, but we need to remember to feed both.

Jesus went up to the top of a mountain and sat down with his disciples. Jesus asked his disciple Philip, "How are we going to feed all these people?" Philip replied, "It would take a LOT of money to buy even a little bread for all of them."

Another one of Jesus' disciples, Andrew, was also with Jesus. He told him that a young boy in the crowd had five loaves of bread and two fish. "But that's certainly not enough for this crowd!" he said. There were over 5,000 people on the mountain. Then Jesus told the disciples to ask the people to sit down. He took the loaves and fish that the young boy had given him. He gave thanks to God and then began to share the food with the crowd. Everyone ate as much as they wanted. When Jesus asked the disciples to gather what was left over, they filled twelve baskets! People were astonished and began to believe in Jesus.

We may not be able to do such astounding miracles as Jesus did. But every time we share what we have with others, we can make our gifts go twice as far than if we kept everything to ourselves.

- When we have extra clothes in our house, we can give some to people who need clothes.
- If we have food in our pantry, we can give some to the food bank.
- When we have toys or candy and our friends don't, we can share with them.

Sometimes it seems as if we would be happier if we kept everything for ourselves. But when we share, not only do we spread happiness to the person with whom we share, we also feel better inside.

Try to think of three things you can share with others, and write them on the lines below. Remember, don't just write down your ideas—make sure you do them!

I can share my ______________________________ with ______________________________.

I can share my ______________________________ with ______________________________.

I can share my ______________________________ with ______________________________.

Receiving Communion

We have GATHERED together with our Christian family. We have LISTENED to God's Word. We have GIVEN THANKS AND PRAISE to God for all God has given us and done for us. We have TOLD THE STORY of Jesus' Last Supper with his friends. We have PRAYED as Jesus taught us to pray. Now it is time for us to RECEIVE HOLY COMMUNION.

Use the word list to fill in the blanks to tell what happens at Communion time.

We all come to the front of the church, where the priest and, if necessary, the Extraordinary Ministers of Holy Communion will be standing. They will hold up the ______________(which we call the host) and say, "The ______________ of ______________." We say, "______________." We take the host and eat it. Then we may go to the minister who has the chalice of______________. They will hold up the chalice and say, "The ______________of ______________." We say, "______________." We take the chalice and drink a small sip. Finally, we return to our seats where we ______________ God for sharing the gift of Jesus with us in holy Communion. We should join in the Communion song and offer a prayer of thanksgiving to God.

Word List: bread Body Christ Amen Blood Christ Amen wine thank

Go in Peace

We have gathered. We have listened. We have given thanks and praise to God. We have offered gifts of bread and wine. We have received the Body and Blood of our Lord. Now it is time for the priest to bless us and send us forth into the world. Now it is time for the real work to begin!

What is our work? We now have to live the Eucharist.

We are to go in peace. We are to love and serve the Lord in one another. Where there is a lonely heart, we can offer our friendship. Where there is someone who is tired, we can help out. Where there is someone who is sad, we can bring joy. Where people are fighting, we can be peacemakers. The ways in which we can love and serve God are as endless as our talents and personalities!

The final part of the liturgy is called the Concluding Rites.

Final Blessing

We pray for God's blessing as we go out into the world to do God's work.

Dismissal

The priest tells us, "Go in peace, glorifying the Lord by your life." We reply, "Thanks be to God."

Recessional Hymn

We join our voices in song. United in faith, we go our separate ways into our families, classrooms, workplaces, and playgrounds. Out into the world, we go forth as disciples of Jesus.

Ritual Connection

The word *Mass* comes from the Latin word *missa.* When we used to pray the liturgy in Latin, the priest would say, *"Ite, missa est,"* which means, "Go, you are sent out." We are not just told the liturgy is over...we are sent out. We have to help make God's reign of justice and peace real in our world each and every day!

Color the picture on the left.

Ritual Connection

At one time, many people had a little font of holy water at the door of their home to remind them to place themselves under God's guidance and protection for the day. Before you leave your house, try saying this prayer: Christ before me, Christ beside me, Christ all around me.

Go forth! Bring Christ to others

Saint Augustine was an African bishop who lived in the early days of the Church. He was so wise that people still talk about his teachings. One of the things he taught people was to "Say Amen to what you are! You are the body of Christ!"

The word *Amen* means "Yes, that is true!" When we say "Amen" after we receive Communion, we are not just saying we believe we are receiving Jesus in the Eucharist. We are also saying we want to become like Jesus. We want to become Jesus' body in the world.

Another famous saint, Teresa of Avila, also understood that Jesus is present in the world in the bodies of his disciples. She taught that people who receive the Body of Christ must also act like the Body of Christ. It is through

our good works that people feel Jesus' love. She wrote, "Christ has no body now on earth but yours, no hands but yours, no feet but yours. Yours are the eyes through which Christ's compassion is to look out to the earth; yours are the feet by which he is to go about doing good; yours are the hands by which he is to bless us now."

Saints among us

Sometimes when someone lives a life modeled on Jesus, the Church calls that person a saint. Not all saints are officially named by the Church. Many wise and holy people live among us. Our friends, neighbors, parents, or teachers could be saints. These people are the Body of Christ to the people they meet. Can you think of someone who lives like Jesus?

Draw or paste a picture of someone you know who has saintly ways.

I think

____

is the Body of Christ in our world because

____

____

____

I will be the hands and feet of Christ

How can you be the Body of Christ? Trace your hand or foot in the box below. Inside your hand or foot, write one or two ways in which you can be the hands, feet, mouth, and eyes of Christ to the people around you.

Go forth! Meet Christ in others

Not only do we *bring* Christ to others, we *meet* Christ in others. In Matthew's Gospel, Jesus tells us about heaven: "Come, you who are blessed by my Father. Inherit the kingdom prepared for you from the foundation of the world. For I was hungry and you gave me food, I was thirsty and you gave me drink, a stranger and you welcomed me, naked and you clothed me, ill and you cared for me, in prison and you visited me."

The people were surprised. They did not remember doing any of those things for Jesus. "Lord, when did we see you hungry and feed you, or thirsty and give you drink? When did we see you a stranger and welcome you, or naked and clothe you? When did we see you ill or in prison, and visit you?" And Jesus told them, "Whatever you did for one of these least brothers of mine, you did for me" (25:34–40). Whenever we help others, we meet Jesus!

Look in a magazine or newspaper for a picture of someone helping a brother or sister in need and paste it here.

Part Two

Memories of My First Eucharist

I CELEBRATED FIRST EUCHARIST ON:

____

THE PEOPLE WHO CAME TO CELEBRATE WITH ME WERE:

____

____

THE TEACHERS, CATECHISTS, OR PRIESTS WHO HELPED ME GET READY FOR MY FIRST EUCHARIST WERE:

____

____

THE THING I LIKED MOST ABOUT MY FIRST EUCHARIST CELEBRATION WAS:

____

____

WE HAD LOTS OF DELICIOUS FOOD ON THE DAY WE CELEBRATED FIRST EUCHARIST. SOME OF THE FOOD I ATE WAS:

____

____

THESE ARE SOME OF THE GIFTS AND KEEPSAKES I RECEIVED:

____

____

NOW THAT I AM MORE FULLY A MEMBER OF GOD'S CHURCH, I HOPE:

____

____

Here are some pictures of me on the day I celebrated my first Eucharist.

Part Three

Parent Pages

INTRODUCTORY PAGES

One way to emphasize that the preparation and celebration of Eucharist is a community rather than an individual event is to have the children prepare with other children in the parish. This process helps families get to know other families in the parish. Have your son or daughter periodically check the list of children preparing for first Eucharist to see if they have met any new children who are also preparing for the sacrament.

PART ONE

Our Journey Begins at Baptism

The goal of this section (p. 5) is to teach children that each of us is on a long journey toward fullness of life in Christ. This journey begins at baptism and never ends. Eucharist, which is the source and summit of the Christian life, is a vital part of our spiritual journey. The focus of these pages is on situating the children in the context of a wider community (saints, godparents, friends, parishioners) of the body of Christ and on reminding them that they are important and cherished members.

At some point during this time of preparation, consider inviting your son or daughter's godparents for a visit and have them recall the events of the day.

God Called You by Name (p. 13): If you do not know the meaning of your child's name, try looking it up in a baby book. Several websites explain what a name means. Visit www.babynamesworld.com for a start.

Bible Stories (p. 16): While you may not have time to look up every story suggested, take the time to look up one or two. This will help familiarize your child (and maybe even you) with the Scriptures.

Jesus Invites You to the Banquet Table

This section (p. 19) introduces the structure of the liturgy (Mass) by comparing it to other celebrations in our lives. The more we understand what we are doing at our celebrations of the Eucharist, the more deeply we will appreciate its meaning and significance in our lives.

We Love to Celebrate (p. 21): Our appreciation of the sacredness of the eucharistic celebration is deepened if we have a sense of the sacredness of all gatherings of family and friends. It is important to make every mealtime special. As life gets busier and busier, even frantic for many people, a relaxed sit-down meal can become a rarity. This year in which you celebrate your child's first Eucharist might be a good time to reorganize family life so that meals are truly family times. Here are a few easy ways to do this that require very little effort:

a) Say or sing grace at every meal.

b) Light candles.

c) Refrain from discussing "issues" at the table so that mealtimes are not times of discipline but, rather, of telling the day's stories.

d) Ask your children interesting questions, such as, "What are you most thankful for today? Who was the most interesting person you met today? What was the funniest moment in your day?"

e) Use the good dishes occasionally.

We Gather Together

In this section (p. 28), the children will learn how the Introductory Rites form us into a community and acknowledge that Christ is present in our midst. They will also learn the importance of the cross as a symbol of our faith.

The Cross/We Have One Another (p. 31): Children, like adults, often have worries and anxieties. It is important to help them develop a sense that they are not alone and that God is always with them, guiding them, upholding them, and strengthening them. One of the most important ways God does this is by giving us sisters and brothers in the Church who will be with us in times of both sorrow and joy.

Learn to Know and Follow Christ (p. 36): This ritual, adapted from the Rite of Christian Initiation, is a good way to pray with your child. You can use some of this blessing ritual as part of your bedtime prayer with your children. In filling in the blanks, your child may need some help figuring out how to follow Christ in each of the various ways. It is perfectly OK to give them suggestions if they cannot come up with them on their own. (For example, "We can keep Jesus in our thoughts by praying, in our ears by listening to our parents, in our eyes by looking at how beautiful God's world and people are," and so forth.)

We Share Sacred Stories

In this section (p. 39), we focus on meeting God the Father, Son, and Holy Spirit, since the entire holy Trinity is revealed in the body of sacred Scripture. One of the best gifts you can give your child is a good children's Bible. The stories of Scripture have been told throughout the ages to pass on insights and wisdom to each generation. They are truly places of encounter with God.

The Sower (p. 42): Download a free expanded version of the Parable of the Sower with discussion questions (along with a scene to draw and color) by visiting Liguori.org/jesus-invites-me-to-the-feast.html. Click on "Parable of the Sower.

One-Minute Meditations (p. 45): This type of prayer works well as a regular part of your family's bedtime routine. It is important to teach children that the voice of God is always an affirming, loving voice. When teaching your child this type of prayer, you can suggest things your child may hear, such as "I love you," "You are mine," "I am proud of you," and "Be kind."

Bible Word Search (p. 49) Answer Key

Y	Y	E	G	A	E	W	P	U	C	H	E	C	D	L
L	T	Y	T	N	C	R	G	S	N	O	B	A	R	E
I	C	S	N	U	I	C	U	O	A	Y	S	N	O	C
M	R	N	E	Q	C	D	L	T	S	L	D	T	W	T
O	E	H	M	I	D	K	A	A	P	P	M	O	S	I
H	E	O	A	K	R	A	M	E	M	I	E	R	D	O
T	D	J	T	L	U	P	C	A	R	A	R	L	O	N
D	N	T	S	B	I	B	L	E	V	T	T	C	G	A
L	L	L	E	R	O	T	C	E	L	N	S	I	S	R
N	E	W	T	E	S	T	A	M	E	N	T	R	O	Y
G	N	I	D	A	E	R	D	N	O	C	E	S	I	N
E	O	Z	L	S	N	O	I	T	I	T	E	P	S	F
P	K	X	O	N	S	Z	M	A	T	T	H	E	W	T
Z	L	U	K	E	F	P	X	W	S	M	X	R	U	X

Finding Your Way in the Bible (p. 51): The references in this puzzle refer to the colors mentioned in the *New Revised Standard Version (NRSV)* of the Bible. If you use another translation *(Good News, New Jerusalem, New American)*, it is possible the puzzle may turn out slightly different. Excellent online Bibles are available at www.Biblestudytools.com and www.BibleGateway.com.

The point of this exercise is to introduce children to the way the Bible is organized. They will not be able to do it without adult assistance. Here are the answers if you get really stuck. But remember, no cheating! Try your Bible first.

Exodus 28:31: You shall make the robe of the ephod all of blue.

Genesis 25:25: The first came out red, all his body like a hairy mantle; so they named him Esau.

Judges 5:10: Tell of it, you who ride on white donkeys, you who sit on rich carpets, and you who walk by the way.

Leviticus 13:32: If...there is no yellow hair in it, and the itch appears to be no deeper than the skin....

Proverbs 16:31: Gray hair is a crown of glory; it is gained in a righteous life.

Exodus 30:4: And you shall make two golden rings for it.

Song of Solomon 2:1: I am a rose of Sharon, a lily of the valleys.

1 Kings 14:23: For they also built...on every high hill and under every green tree.

Matthew 16:2: He answered them, "When it is evening, you say, 'It will be fair weather, for the sky is red.'"

Luke 16:19: There was a rich man who was dressed in purple and fine linen.

Revelation 1:13: I saw one like the Son of Man, clothed with a long robe and with a golden sash across his chest.

Lamentations 4:5: Those who were brought up in purple cling to ash heaps.

Numbers 33:10: They set out from Elim and camped by the Red Sea.

Exodus 39:31: They tied to it a blue cord, to fasten it on the turban above; as the LORD had commanded Moses.

Genesis 1:30: I have given every green plant for food.

Ecclesiastes 9:8: Let your garments always be white; do not let oil be lacking on your head.

Leviticus 13:30: If it appears deeper than the skin and the hair in it is yellow and thin.

We Share a Sacred Meal

In this section (p. 52), the children will learn about the central part of the liturgy. This is where we encounter the risen Lord in Communion.

Foot Washing (p. 57): Download a free story about a woman who washed Jesus' feet (along with a scene to color) by visiting Liguori.org/jesus-invites-me-to-the-feast.html. Click on "Jesus and the Woman."

Bread Baking (p. 60): Baking bread is a wonderful way to involve the whole family in a conversation about Eucharist. If you have a family recipe for bread, use it instead of the recipe suggested in the book.

We Give Thanks and Praise (p. 61): Developing an "attitude of gratitude" is one of the most important things we can help our children do to become healthy and happy adults. Our culture of consumerism develops in us feelings of dissatisfaction with what we have so that we will buy more and more things. Unfortunately, this tends to make us very unhappy people. Some people will always have more than we do. But for the most part, we are very fortunate and blessed. The more we are able to count our blessings and live in thankfulness, the happier we will all be in the long run.

The Lord's Prayer (p. 63): If your child does not know the Lord's Prayer, they should now learn it by heart.

Loaves and Fishes (p. 64): If you would like to read more Bible stories about feeding, here are a few suggestions:

> **Exodus 16–17:7:** God feeds the Israelites in the desert.
>
> **1 Kings 17:8–16:** A poor woman shares her food with a prophet and has more than enough.
>
> **Luke 10:38–42:** Jesus eats with his friends Martha and Mary.
>
> **Luke 19:2–8:** Jesus eats with a sinner.
>
> **Luke 24:13–35:** The disciples recognize Jesus in the breaking of the bread.
>
> **John 2:1–11:** Jesus helps at a wedding feast.
>
> **John 6:28–35:** Jesus is the Bread of Life.

How to Receive Communion (p. 66): It is very important to practice the etiquette of receiving Communion with your child. Reverence does not necessarily come naturally to children. It usually needs to be taught.

Go in Peace

The aim of this section (p. 67) is to help children understand that simply to receive Eucharist without trying to live as eucharistic people is insufficient. We must take our faith into the world and do our part to help make the kingdom of God present in the lives of the people we meet.

Saints Among Us (p. 71): This is a good time to tell more stories of the saints. Liguori's *Saints and Me!* series includes more than 35 beautifully illustrated children's books about saints. Visit Liguori.org//for-everyone/popular-series/saints-and-me-series.html.

PART TWO

Memories of My First Eucharist

Use the remainder of the journal to help your child create memory pages about his or her first Eucharist celebration.